DIRGES FOR MY HOMELAND

A collection of war and other poems

BY

Saah Charles N'Tow

First published by AuthorHouse 06/16/04

ISBN: 1-4184-2031-X (e-book)
ISBN: 1-4184-2030-1 (Paperback)

Library of Congress Control Number: 2003099775

This book is printed on acid free paper.

Printed in the United States of America
Bloomington, IN

Dedication

My thanks and praises to God Almighty and all
who made this book possible

Table of Contents

Preface

Violence always arrives as a surprise-an unwelcome and ultimately unexpected guest. After all who would willingly wait to bear such company? The truth is that war becomes a reality not when it is in the next country, or county, or village, but when it knocks at your neighbor's door and casts its shadow across the hearth of you and yours. It is as if violence is so unbelievable—so outrageous a possibility--that it must be touched to be believed. Scholars of wars and violence will tell you that those who flee violence take flight *after* experiencing its outrages more often than they do to avoid experiencing it altogether. And those who have experienced war at the wrong end of the gun will tell you that the outrage can never be prepared for.

Much like war this work ill bears any prefacing. It is an immersion in cold realities and hot blood. Like staccato from the AK-47's that unsilently haunt its lines, these poems expose the reader to the naked terror and twisted logic of wartime violence—suddenly, and without introduction. Neighbors and friends may become one's killers, while strangers may become shareholders in misery and long suffering. Children learn that victims are merely those who fail to victimize. Lives are bartered for canned food at checkpoints. Innocence and guilt can be found at both ends of the gun.

This is a baptism the author is sanctified to administer—those who have tread the valley of the shadow of death are indeed perhaps the only ones who can speak of it without exploiting the suffering within. Those who walk through war scapes and survive are branded forever as "witness". These poems are just this--a bearing of witness—at once both transcendent and grounded—an appeal to a nation, and a testimony to the checkpoint. There is no cooking of the books in this accounting—warlords, the makers of child soldiers, the exile leaders who bicker at peace instead of building it, and the indifferent citizen half a world away unwilling to disturb his comfortable ignorance or pay 10 cents more a gallon for gas in order to save a million souls on a different continent—the author audits us all.

However the author also bears witness to the fact that though assaulted by war life may yet continue to defy it—often by insisting on the imperative of the seemingly mundane. Love and longing haunt both those who leave and those left behind. And there is perhaps hope, if it is found to also haunt the soldier. I have known the author of these poems for several years now—long enough to know of his own hope—a hope that nourishes his deep and abiding commitment to the peace and healing of his war-torn homeland of Liberia. These poems are but another act of voice in his call for a difficult peace— not only difficult because it seems so hard to achieve, but because in order to last it must be more than the termination of violence. This is a calling for the participation of the voiceless and committed to the belief that without the guidance of the aspirations of everyday people, politics is merely the mindless and dangerous accumulation of power. The leadership of peace seeks to listen rather than to speak, to learn rather than dictate, and to respond rather than to levy its own desires.

Violence is the only true preface to a dirge. A summary of sadness, a dirge may also be a call to end the senselessness that violence is…and thus may itself be a preface to peace. Pray it be so.

Stephen C. Lubkemann, PhD
Assistant Professor of Anthropology
George Washington University

Dirges for my Homeland
A collection of Liberian War and other poems by: Saah N'Tow

Reflections: The Beginning

As the truth we dreaded most unfolded

We could no longer ignore reality

There was a war

It was deadly

It was a civil war

Even worse

Once crowded streets

Now stood empty

Soldiers' checkpoints

Surfaced everywhere

Litters of corpses

Lie unburied

Our beautiful city

Was now lost to war

Nights grew longer and colder

Sound of the guns

Now music in the air

Angry soldiers

Shouting orders

Terrified victims

Begging and pleading

The fear of death now

Worse than death itself

Terror was now a regular guest

Trust now a thing of the past

Friends or foes

There was no telling apart

An enemy from afar

Is easy to fight

But our enemies were close

We knew they were once our friends

Who knew our inside out

So home for us became

Anywhere else but home

A Cold Encounter

HALT! We heard in the distance
Myself, my wife, my child, we stood
No one offered any resistance
The reasons obvious, we understood

A man emerged from the blanket of darkness
A gun, a knife and loads of munitions
The face we saw was the face of coldness
We understood, so we offered no temptation

The True Frontier

The frontier stands beyond
Beyond the gaze of the naked eyes
The naked eyes see a no man's land
Filled with wreckage of buildings
And piles of scattered corpses of fallen victims
The naked eyes see the barricade of ruins
They see the killing fields,
Soaked with the blood of unarmed and innocent civilians

They see the relics of towns and villages long destroyed
And the decaying corpses of helpless
And innocent women and children
The naked eyes see fighters and their guns
They see mindless soldiers and leaders
Vicious and greedy
Searching, robbing and
Abusing shattered families
Frantically fleeing to safety
But, the true frontier lies deep within

Beyond the gaze of the naked eyes
It's the greed for power and wealth
The thoughtlessness

The blind rage

The hatred

It's the pain of humiliation

The lusting for revenge

The envy, the gossips

The treachery, the lies and deceits

The true frontier is deep within

Beyond the gaze of the naked eyes

Smoke Screens

When smoke screens of lies and deception cloud the truth
Trusting hearts and minds are always misled
When fake reports are used as proof
The truth is delayed but it'll have its day

When a bag of rice can pay for a people's vote
And conscience is detained and has no space
Those who vote must take serious note
Rich or poor everyone has one vote

When any conditions threaten the freedom to choose
And the right to vote is a warrant of death
The WILL to resist, we must not loose
Because in union strong, we will not fail

Harsh Realities

We heard the sound: it was horrible
Then the scream, someone in pain, a moan
The scream grew faint, no longer audible
The sound of a gun, a dying man left to moan

We couldn't help: we were captives
Painful and true, the reality of impotence
In anguish and grief, revenge was our motive
But we grieved in vain with raging hate in silence

The sound was the same, always horrible
Sometimes a scream: sometimes dead silence
Always death and a pool of blood
With hate and greed the raging pestilence

Who will be next, the victim to die?
Who will stand aside, to wait his turn?
Who will want to help, yet run to hide?
Who will force a smile, yet in anger burn?

Saah Charles N'Tow

Through The Bushes

Journey painful, hard and long
In search of dear life, they must carry on
For the young, the old and all who fled
It was through the bushes that all roads led

Death and pain and infliction of suffering, untold
For the unfortunate: the weak, the strong, the young and old
Trekking wearily on a journey long
Through the bushes: wet, dark, thick and strong

Sudden departures, cautious and slow
To destinations unknown and fate unsure
Shattered families creeping and crawling
Through the bushes towards safety's calling

Wango's Wisdom

My Son,
Hate divides, fear weakens
And greed pollutes the fragrance of progress
But resistance, popular, honest and true
Will crush the forces of evil
No matter how strong

Harmless are weapons without users
For left alone, triggers cannot pull themselves
Dangerous is the one with hate and malice
For hate is blind and like a flame
It'll never die
Because, hate has no grave
And malice will not easily fade

Complacency is the bedrock of reluctance
And reluctance breeds fear
Fear paralyzes a people's progress
To freedom and democracy

Saah Charles N'Tow

But power to a people

Who stand united in resistance

With persistence

For evil knows no triumph

'Cause evil is never satisfied

No, not ever,

My son

Arduous Pleasure

She now holds a Child:
Borne into an angry world
To a union that never was
A son that unites the two
From a crime of sex too cruel

It was his pleasure
To steal her most valued treasure
In his moment of lustful madness
That became her life long memory of sadness
He was overpowered and obsessed by lust
No love, no feelings, a betrayal of unspoken trust

Tinted by hate, big and strong, he had no fear
Useless to struggle
Unable to scream,
She lies in her pool of tears
She surrendered.

Saah Charles N'Tow

The day my sun went down

One bright sunny day
Of peace and calm
I saw dark clouds
Of hate begin to form

I watched helplessly
As they cruelly and slowly
Covered my joy
As I shivered
From the chills
Of the wicked winds

I froze
At the sound
Of the threatening thunder
In the distance
For when my day began
It was a sunny one
Now it's all gray and dull
The forecast said
Rain it would not
Shining bright
The sun would be

No chilling winds
Or distant thunder
But a mighty fine one
My day would be
It's like going to Heaven
But getting stuck
In the clouds
Yes the clouds
The chilly white clouds
Disappointingly cold

Bad News

Courage
Doesn't live here anymore
No not since terror
And fear moved in

Hope is unwillingly
Leaving town
To make space
For threat and force

And weary old resistance
Can longer deny
His inapt defeat
To suppression

Poor trust was evicted
And publicly flogged
By the armies of
Lies
Deceits
And shame

Though bravery was tempted

To stay and fight

It was fright

That took up the offer instead

Chaos now lives

Where peace

Once lived

Hatred now sleeps

In the bed

That once belonged to love

Sanity's land

Has been taken

By madness

While Hypocrisy

Now spends time

In almost every home

The Head of the town

Is no longer

The good Law

For the tyrant Crime

Took over

And killed him

Saah Charles N'Tow

In what was a bloody coup

Respect was spotted
Frantically fleeing her home
Because Insult
Her archrival
Was desperately trying
To find and kill her
Good old Education
Now lives in exile
In a distant land
Using her skills
And knowledge
To build some strange new land

While the family of ignorance
Happily lives in her house
Next door to
The families of
Stupidity
Madness
And hate

Death
Is now a special guest

He comes

And goes

From time

To time

Hunger

Frustration

Humiliation

Suffering

And pain

Are the specialists employed

To make sure

Death comes again

And again and again...

Saah Charles N'Tow

The Massacre

In the camp, they've all gathered
The rich, the poor, the beggars and thieves
Fleeing the war, they must live together
Christians, Moslem, whatever their beliefs

In the cold of the night
Messengers of death walk
With guns and knives and power might
And declaring might is right
They're hunters of flesh and killers of the weak

Innocent and unaware, they sleep
Mothers and fathers, brothers and sisters
They sleep deep, but terror creeps
They sleep in comfort to wake no more

Death arrives, berserk and unflinching
Blades and bullets, tearing and killing
Headless corpses, corpse-less heads, MURDER!
Wanton and unparalleled, murder most disgusting

The Checkpoint

The smell of death filled the air

As we joined the queue to be searched

We couldn't help but think in fear

That the corpses around could soon be us

But, we made it through the Checkpoint, alive!

We were stopped like all the rest

We were searched like the others

But unlike many before and after us

We weren't killed; we were left to live

So, we made it through the Checkpoint, alive!

No one left the Checkpoint the same

No one was immune to its effects

There was fear and there was humiliation

There was helplessness and there was pain

There was uncertainty, but somehow, there was hope

That's why we made it through the checkpoint, alive!

Pain and more pain

Arms and legs plotting to betray

Fading strength

Signs of the troubles ahead

Countless wounds

Broken body

Broken spirit

Pain, pain and more pain

My tomato or my life?

The trek to freedom was a path filled with troubles and trials
Food was a problem, strength was an issue and hope was fading fast
Although we knew not where our destiny led
We were determined as ever to get to the other side

I was determined to complete the journey with
At least one of my tomato cans
Twelve tomato cans at the start of the journey, now reduced to one
One at the final check-point, I lost the rest to as many check-point
guards
This one was mine, with it I will not part, not if I could help it

The routine search was complete,
But the can was separated from the rest of my clothes
I had seen this before for that was how the rest were taken from me.
Oh no, not this time, this tomato, I had to keep

This soldier would not budge because
He too was determined ~ determined as I was
This soldier: he was mean and he was tough
A soldier with a strange sense of humor
For he simply tapped me on my shoulder and asked me to stand and
look

Saah Charles N'Tow

At the end of his pointed finger was a condemned man waiting to be
shot

Two soldiers were debating who would kill this one
While the condemned man watched, knowing his life was no longer
his own
Now the soldier who searched my bags did not say much,
But with a killer's smile
He simply asked me this ~ "It this where you want to be?"

I took one last look at my tomato can and then at the condemned man
I knew it was courtesy for the soldier
To even give me a choice in the matter
I knew it was time: sadly, it was time to give up my fight
So without a struggle I chose to live and let my tomato die

Choice?

No one leaves was the order

He or she who tries to leave is the enemy

The enemy must die

Enemy of the state must be killed

Stay and be ruled by the hands of terror

Stay and flirt with danger and death

Stay and wait for the next order

Stay and face uncertainty and fear

Or meet your fate in flight

Part II

The Child Soldier

His hand is always on the trigger
His tiny fingers ever so ready to squeeze
High on drugs and his new found power
He is a child, but he brings pain
He is weak but he is death
He is indifferent but causes severance
He is innocent but brings destruction
He suffers but he brings suffering
To the victims at the end of his gun

The child soldier is a victim of greed
An instrument of death for heartless warlords
He is vulnerable as are his victims
He is disposable as are those he disposes
He fears them as they fear him
He is helpless as they are helpless
He is hopeful, yet hopeless
To his bosses, he is expendable
Yet he is despised
By the victims at the end of his gun

Jungle Justice

The face of innocence
The heart of a killer
The age of ignorance
He is a little child soldier
But for the gun
He is only a child
He is one: the judge and jury
He is the plaintiff and the executioner

He is one: the truth and the lie
He holds life and death in his tiny little hands
High on his new found power
He pulls the trigger and it's your last hour

Jungle justice in a dirt town dusty
The child, a trigger-happy soldier
Holds a single barrier gun, rusty
One wrong word or move and it's all over

In the thick of the jungle dark and deep
This is your fate: it is decided
Witnessed by trees and your fading shadow
You have no chance for an appeal
BOOM! And it's shattered dreams

Little Boy Soldier

Little Boy Soldier, for big power
Crazy Soldier boy, high on drugs
Crazy little killers, going mad
Can't stop killing, but afraid to die

Wicked men for money,
Have turned your head
Against your brothers,
Your sisters and all
They have made you blind
And made you destroy
Now open your eyes
And see what you have done

They promised you money
And power as well
They promised to educate
And protect you too
But are you now better
Than before they came?
Little boy soldier,
You are worse now than then

Today, you are an addict,
A thief and a killer
You have killed your teachers
And burned down your schools
Who will teach you now?
You have killed them all
Where will you learn?
You have destroyed it all

When you walk by day,
People flee
When you sleep at night,
Your victims you see
Now you think you are stuck
And just can't stop
But little boy soldier,
O yes you can

Yes Little boy soldier,
There is still hope
The chance to be
A good boy again
But you must lay down your arms
And learn to trust
To trust and love
And be human again

Saah Charles N'Tow

The Unwilling Soldier

To survive, he must become a soldier
To be a soldier, he must become a killer
Weapons of death must ride upon his shoulders
Full of hate, he'll become a brutal and ruthless killer

Transfixed, he watched, numb with confusion
Unable to understand, consumed by fear
To watch perhaps brings much less tension
Than the feeling of guilt, he must come to bear

The victim: a woman, an innocent mother
Helpless and frantic, she's pleading for compassion
Helpless and afraid, he must watch the murder
The brutal act, he too must learn to perfection

Killing to live and living to kill
Controlled by fear, no one to trust
Lingering wars that'll give him thrill
A thrill to kill, a lust for blood

Friends before will now be his foes
His victims of hate, prejudice and abuse
Threat and force now access to food
When he makes demands, they will not refuse

The Foolish Fighter

You foolish fighter,

I bet you think you are a soldier,

Fighting for the rights to your land;

Defending bravely and fighting,

To restore honor and joy,

To bring back justice,

And the freedom you once enjoyed.

You crazy fighter,

I bet you think you are the good guy;

Killing off all the bad guys,

Burning down their towns,

Killing their children,

And raping their daughters and wives.

You dumb fighter,

I bet you think you deserve a medal;

For your gallantry,

Your sacrifices,

Your bravery,

Your heroism.

And stupidity

AFL, NPFL, ULIMO - J or K,

Or whatever you call yourself.

You are no more than a plain old fool;

To think you are a soldier;

Who deserves a medal?

And one who should be proud.

O foolish fighter,

How foolish can you be?

To think you are a soldier;

Fighting for peace and prosperity,

As you tear to pieces,

The very fabrics of our society

O foolish fighter,

Where is bravery in destruction?

Where is gallantry in rape?

Where is sacrifice in atrocity?

Where is heroism in banditry?

O foolish fighter,

Be not deceived, whoever you are.

You too are dying like those you kill.

For every bullet you fire;

Every person you kill,

And every home you destroy.

You are killing the human in you,

And destroying the very land you claim to defend

O foolish fighter,

You are a stooge and not a soldier.

You are a victim not a hero.

Because you are fighting your own,

Destroying your own land,

Killing those you once loved and cared for.

O foolish Liberian fighter,

When this cloud of madness finally clears,

And you finally come to your senses.

You'll find that you've killed yourself,

And find that you've destroyed your land;

Your MOTHERLAND;

The land your fathers fought so hard to build.

O foolish fighter,

When the dust is cleared,

You will find that you're left alone;

Alone to face your nightmares and fears;

Alone to rebuild your land;

And alone to mourn your loss.

Only then will you know the truth;

About how blind your loyalty was.

You mindless Liberian fighter,

How big a fool can you be?

Your families stay in the war and die,

But the warlords' families flee and live abroad.

They feed you with hate,

Supply you with arms,

But they feed on the goods you loot.

O mad fighter,

How long will it take to realize,

That they don't give a damn about you?

You are a fool; nothing but a stooge.

To them: the warlords, you're a foot stool;

A pawn in their game of chess;

A lamb they can sacrifice;

A simple madman with no name;

A fool no more than a yes-man.

True Soldiers

When in ages past, we heard of soldiers true
We pretended in play that we were soldiers too
Because then we were proud of our soldiers
Smartly dressed with their guns on their shoulders

They were true soldiers, our nation's defence
Against our common enemies, our nation's offence
Noble and strong, they stood prepared
To protect and defend, they felt compelled

The laws of the land, they swore to uphold
To protect the land, they were ready and bold
True soldiers they were, marching proud in their strides
Displaying our flag and its beautiful stripes

The true soldiers we knew never turned on their own
Never were guilty of rape or burning down a town
The true soldiers we knew always defended life
Never looted a home or robbed our nation's wealth

The true soldiers' lives were structured and stern
And their honor and pride were the stripes that they earned
Lusts and greed were never a part of their plans
For they respected the lives of those placed in their hands

Saah Charles N'Tow

Evil

I have seen the face of evil

It is dark, creepy, scary and bedeviled

A face with phony smiles

Twisted thoughts, with countless secrets to hide

Every so often it wears a mask of smiles

Ever so ready to tell a pack of lies

Evil is selfish, devious and shrewd

It hurts, it ruins, and does not matter who

On the ruins of others, evil feeds

Temptation and corruption, evil breeds

Evil is greedy, dark and deep

Restless and unflinching, evil never sleeps

Evil does not defend; it offends

It does not amuse, it confuses

It never helps, but always hurts

Evil connives and never unites

Wango, my [s]hero

Wango my [s] hero never once wore an amour

Never once owned or handled a gun

She never led an uprising

Or made a public speech in rebellion

Wango my [s] hero

She only took care of me

Never once left my side

Wango cared for me

Never once turned her back

Wango II

She braved the stormy weather

Baked in the scorching sun

She froze in the chilly winter

But never once gave up on me

Wango! Wango! Smile if you can hear me

Shake the trees or trouble the waters

Send us some gentle winds

Or give us a sign to let us know you hear us

Wango III

On the occasion of your untimely visit

My heart weeps with tears of sadness

My heart weeps with tears of joy

You my son have come home

But your home lies in ruins

From unspeakable terrors

That has caused us unparalleled sorrow

We rejoiced when we heard of your good fortune

How you brought us pride in your achievements

But we cannot rejoice now

No, we cannot rejoice

There are no cattle to sacrifice

There are no fruits or food for a feast

There are no musicians or dancers to celebrate

Strange men came and stole those from us

Don't look for your sisters to come and welcome you

Don't look for your brothers to show you around

Some can see you from the dark corners of their hideouts

Some lie still beneath the dust of the ground we now stand on

Strange men came and destroyed our land

Strange men came and stole our children

Saah Charles N'Tow

Strange men came and defiled our culture

Strange men have stolen our joy

Strange men have awakened our fury

Strange men have forced us to run and hide

Strange men have forced us to lie

To steal, to prostitute ourselves

To kill others

And to die

Wango IV

On the occasion of your untimely visit, my son

I embrace you, I welcome you and I bless you

I am grateful to God for the chance to see you now

But for your peace and the future of our people

I now must bid you farewell with blessing

Son, I must ask you to leave

Before the same strange men come

This time to steal you away from me

Wango V

I bless you now my son

Son of my son: the eldest and future of our clan

You will go and God will help you find

You will see destinations we could only dream of

God will guide you in your sojourn

God will bless you in your quest

You will seek out new opportunities for our survival

You will make new friends to sustain our existence

You will travel to places unknown to explore new chances

You will live so that we too might live through you

You will succeed to help our clan revive

P/s: Wango is my Grandma - the mother of my father, who was there for me in the thick of the struggle. Her words of wisdom ring in my ears, though she's departed for the great beyond. This poem was written as a tribute to Wango. It is written in this form so that Wango lives through her words of wisdom. I love and miss Wango. Peace be to her ashes.

Fools and Stooges

The hand that pulls the trigger
Is a hand being pulled by a string
By the puppet master much, much higher
The hand of the face unseen

Moving lenses, hidden scenes
Roving microphones, unheard sounds
Fools and stooges as instruments of death
A fool's madness, someone's last breath

White collar killers: greedy businessmen
Shipment of weapons, mass of corpses
Bombs and missiles, buried cities
Countless corpses, business transactions

Creating hunger, creating poverty
Breeding hatred, the setting of crime
Scarce essentials, competition intense
Angered by hunger, driven to kill

The puppet master's trickery
Fools and stooges delight
Fighting over little things,

Saah Charles N'Tow

While the master takes it all

Fools and stooges, destroy their homes
They destroy their people and destroy their land
But the puppet master clever builds his home elsewhere
He steals the loots and flees to a distant land

Now the fools and stooges must rebuild their land
They must mend their broken pieces
And they must heal their wounds
They live in the mess he made them to make
While he seeks asylum in the land of the rich with their riches

Shadows

Shadows, shadows, shadows
Shadows whenever it is bright
Shadows wherever there is light

When your life my friend is shining bright
With the beam of success and its glistening lights
Beware my friend! Beware!
Cause, somewhere behind
And still lingering on
There is still darkness in your light
It is the darkness of your past
Your shadow dark of failures and grief
The phantom of your worries and pains

Shadows, shadows, shadows
Shadows wherever you go
In your light
Your shadow will show
In your darkness
It is there
But cannot be seen

Saah Charles N'Tow

Shadows will always follow
Shadows will never go away
It is like a little rain
When the sun is hot

It is like a plain white sheet
With a little dark spot
Shadow is like feeling down
When you are somehow glad
Shadow is like feeling good
When you are doing something bad
Shadow is like being in the heat
And still feeling cold

Ghangay[1] like kae[2]

You like kae Jacko

You na like kae Jacko lanta

You like kae Ghangay

You na like Ghangay like kae

We joined the singing

Our wary legs sending us signals of fatigue,

begging our bodies to stop

Our stomachs making those familiar sounds of hunger

With our eyelids plotting to betray us by shutting

We had no choice but to join the crowd

We did not liked it but Ghangay did

We had to sing along

The news was great that day for the dancing crowd

All fighters loyal to Charlie Ghangay Taylor

They were singing because President Doe was just killed

We had no choice but to celebrate

We did not like it but the singing crowd in Gbanga[3] did

---

[1]Ghangay is the nickname of former President Charles G. Taylor

[2] "Like Kae" is a local Liberian way of saying "likes it" in the context used.

[3] Gbanga is the capital city of Bong County ~ a county in Liberia

We had to sing and dance

Our weakening hearts hoping for the end

Our limited minds making ready for peace

With the last of our fading strength

We shouted and danced along

Like many including the fighters in the crowd

We believed it was the end but Ghangay did not

When we are the enemy

When we are the enemy

We are the victims of the weapons fired by our hands

We are the losers of our peace and unity

We are the cowards blinded by hate to the wisdom of peace

We are the destroyers of our most cherished prize: ourselves

We are the abusers

We are the accusers

We are the looters

We cause the explosions

We bring about the destruction

We become the killers

We are the victims

When we are the enemy

Part III

Saah Charles N'Tow

The Unknown s/heroes

No one remembers their names

Not one of them made claim to fame

But they bled and they died

Just like the heroes we knew

They lie deceased

So that we may live in peace

No one remembers their last words

Not one of them left traces

Of anything to record

Yet they lie unburied and real,

Just like the heroes we knew

They lost their stories

To the pages of history

No one saw them nurse their wounds

Not one of them is known

To have made a sound

Even in death, no one saw them

And no one knew them

They swallowed their pain

To help us dream

Reflections: Mama's Child Lives

Away from pain
And into pain
A sudden departure, cruelly ordained
A gap of distance, a bridge of fear, and
Hurts and pain and tears of detachment.

Mama's image, befogging fast
But Mama's farewell still echoes loudly
To flee from death, Mama said
Is no assurance that you would live
But a final recourse, my child
A chance to fight for life

For I'd rather live, she said
With the hope of knowing
That somewhere
Somehow, you live
Than to know you're dead
To know you'll walk no more
Mama shared no tears
Mama showed no fear

But she wore a smile, a neurotic smile

A tight embrace: yet

Gentle and warm

With faith in GOD

And a fervent hope

That soon the war will end, and

Our time apart will not be long

Guns, everywhere clamor of war

Grown ups die

Mama's children watch and learn

In fear of death

But with a will to live

Mama's children

Borne to an angry world

Their childhood lost to violence

Killing for survival

Killing for fun

Mama waits in an angry world

Where compassion is a stranger

A guest unknown

An act in reality that

Never comes, while

Hate and greed together

Rule the minds of men

Mama waits, but doubts

She's no longer smiling

She's no longer hopeful

It's been days

It's been weeks and months

Now, years and years

Mama's fears now bring tears

Mama waits but now wonders

If the threat of death still hangs,

Mama no longer believes, but prays

That Mama's child lives

Away from home,

Away from her

A stranger in another world

But still lives

Cease-fire or Peace at last?

Is this cease-fire or peace at last?
Will this new promise be fulfilled?
Or be broken like the rest?
Will tomorrow see the
dawn of lasting peace?
Or is it yet another
scheme to buy more time?
Is this another time to rest?
Treat the sick and bury the dead
Recruit more, buy more arms
And fortify positions

Is it a time to sell more gold
Sell more diamonds
Seek more support
Evacuate warlords' families
Stir up trouble
And start the fight again?
Or is this truly the end?
Is this that time we've all prayed for?
When we can all come home

To a gun free country

To a democracy real and true

Free of warlords, mad and cruel

When our children will not know violence

When the guns will not rule us

Or be harassed by trigger-happy youngsters

Or be the targets of fighters out of control

Or watch helplessly as looting fighters help themselves

To the little that's left of the nothing we have?

Saah Charles N'Tow

Symbu

When the tunnel's light is growing dim
And the darkness around still lingers on
When all it seems, is too much to bear
Do not despair, because Symbu dear
I'll be there for you

When no mortal man or woman will understand
When none is willing your pains to share
When in an abyss of loneliness you find yourself
O Symbu dear, please hang in there
I'll be there for you

When in the midst of these you must share some tears
When there is a dying need for a listening ear
Or you need someone to listen to
Look no further, because Symbu dear
I'll be there for you

Through the thick and thin of your worries and troubles
In your shadows dark of resentment and confusion
As you reconstruct your broken pieces
Symbu honey, please take it easy
I'll be there for you

Symbu II

Tonight my heart
Has boarded the plane of love
It has traveled across
The sea and braved the clouds above
Searching and hunting and
Desperately wanting you, just you
To fill my emptiness in
This valley of a distance so cruel

Tonight the memories
Of our times together have come alive
Like it did yesterday,
The day before and everyday,
Since the day I saw you leave
I hold your hands and kiss your lips
I even talk to and dance with you
I see those happy times we shared and
Even the terrible times we went through

Tonight like every night of late
I feel stronger and stronger
I'll always grow
For somehow in this gap of distance

Saah Charles N'Tow

My desire for you will never grow old

With each passing day

I want you more and more and even more

This distance my love has

Strengthened my desire and time only makes it grow

Lamenting the Full Moon

If only I could share your peace

Your calm

Your serenity

If only I could manage a smile that glitters like yours

If my smiles could melt my shadows of despair

O full moon, my troubled life would be fulfilled

Tell me your secrets, O full moon

Tell me how come you smile still?

Amidst the pain

Amidst the worries

Amidst the frustration of our troubled world

Amidst the horror of our dying planet

Where do you go when it is day?

When greed begins his reign

And terror begins to roam

When corruption stands in the way of progress?

How come you sit and silently watch

As evil works to the beam of your light

Why do you smile and lend your light to thieves

To Killers

To Looters

To muggers

And all who plot to rid us of our land?

I'm a victim too!

I am a face
The faces of the many you do not see
I am the face of one
One of the many
Buried beyond your camera's lens

I am a voice
The voices you do not hear
I am the voice
One of the many
Lost behind your radio frequencies

I am a place
The places you do not go
I am the place
One of the many
Fading beyond your photographer's camera

I am a corpse
The corpses you know as numbers
I am in your reports
Statistics on your sheets
I am the corpse, one of the many

Lying unburied

Rotting from the violence of hatred and war

I am a story

One of your many News stories

Stories you sometimes read

Stories you sometimes watch

All my years of pain

All my years of suffering

All my years of frustration

Flashing by on your screen in a few seconds

And summed up in a few chosen words

I am a target

I am the targets that bring you money

One of the many

The target of the weapons you sell to my killers

Of the missiles you send that leave my villages buried

Of your background sabotage

Of your business deals that stand even at the peril of my life

I am the face you do not see

I am the voice you do not hear

I am the place you cannot go

I am beyond your television screen

I am beyond your radio frequencies

But, I am real

Because, I am a victim too

Saah Charles N'Tow

***

Even the dawn of day

Warns the darkness of his coming

He sends his gentle

Yet powerfully piecing and chilly morning breeze

He releases the morning midst

To awaken the sleeping savannah green

Gently and slowly

He ushers in his light to fill the gap left behind by darkness

***

Peace

Because at last I've heard that you'd come
Time it seems has somehow stood still
My hopes are high, but my fears persist
And I wonder if really you would come

I've heard this time you'd come to stay
But uncertainty has kept my joy at bay
For I've heard this so many times
My feet are sore and I can dance no more

Is it true that you would come?
Will you come this time for real?
Shall I sound the drums and make ready for feast?
Or are you merely crying wolf again?

When at last I'm sure that you would come
I pray that God would give me strength
To sing the victory songs of old
To join the living and dance
To rejoin my family and friends
And forget my sorrow for a while

Saah Charles N'Tow

Still Talking Peace

Fresh smoke spirals in the distance
Smell of flesh and blood still fills the air
Groans and moans echo still
People unarmed are being slaughtered, still
While the men responsible are still talking peace

My village and my people, are held hostages still
My boys and men are still being killed
My women and children are being abused
My people continue to live in terror and fear,
While the men responsible are still talking peace

My people and my country are still being destroyed
Shiploads of weapons are still being bought
Innocent villagers are being massacred still
Food and water are still in short supply
While the men responsible are still talking peace.

My country's wealth is still being swindled
And uncompromising demands are still being made
The hope of peace still lies in the distance
Now in this foreign land, as I linger and wait
I wonder, do the men responsible really want peace?

When it is calm again

The storm has ceased, but it is raining still
The thunders roar and lighting flash
The ground is firm, but it is slippery and wet
Soon the rain will stop and it will be dry again

A storm so sudden and strangely cruel
Will one day cease, but will never die
The pain and anguish it has caused
We may forgive, but will never forget

When it is dry again, we will rise and search
For friends and families and lost loved ones
But who amongst them will be there to find?
What damages are there have we yet to know?

When it is dry again, we will build new homes
Start new families and make new friends
But to the memories of those we've lost
We will remember the storm, even when it is calm

Saah Charles N'Tow

Until this River Dries

A river now fills the gap that separates us

A river wide
A river violent
A river shallow
It is a river filled with the debris of our hate and pain
A river smelling with the foulness of our sins and crimes

It is a river that sings to us songs of our past
With lyrics of woeful evidence of our madness, deception and shame
It is a river that brings us dire warnings for tomorrow
Warnings of what destruction our greed can bring

It is a river dark, suspicious and ironically calm
Quietly flowing with the current of our want for revenge
It is a river that widens with our deceits and lies
A river that thrives on the blood of our innocent families and friends

Until this river dries, we in Liberia will know no peace
Until the debris of our hate turns into forgiveness and love
Until we stop spilling the blood that makes it grow
Until we question the restrictions that bring to focus our affiliations

Or challenge the blanket judgments that raise doubts about our rights

to live and live freely

Until this river's height sinks to levels that reveal

The true power of democracy

When our legislators and judges are no longer

Puppets of a corrupt regime

Until the voice of the press can be heard without restrictions

Until it's mass clears to reveal the riches of our land, hidden deep

Exposing the thugs and thieves who thrive on our people's suffering

Until this river dries, our fear will not die

Until this river dries, our joy will not return

Until this river dries, peace will elude us

Our hurts will not go away

No! No! No! We will not know peace or calm

Until this river dries

Saah Charles N'Tow

Dirges for my homeland

It has been hard and it has been long

We have lost our way and it has all gone wrong

Dark and angry clouds now linger above

Waiting to soak with rain any hope of a peaceful resolve

We are a people scattered in a minefield of vengeance

A minefield of vengeance and revenge

Using everything and anything we can find

To make our killing splurge more profound

Brothers against brothers: reigns of terror and blind hatred

Driven by greedy warlords masquerading as patriots

Shattered families nervously fleeing in all directions

Weary and hopeless searching for divine protection

So-called fighters bringing destruction but promising reconstruction

Promising fairness while dwelling in lies and deception

Talking about freedom,

but they hold our people hostage

Making promises of restoration

but leaving a legacy of poverty

The passing years have taught us well,

the thorny realities of lies and trust

When friendships turned to bloody feuds and

killers turned preachers to save lost souls

When thieves are trusted to enforce the law and

mothers abandon all they hold dear

We've suffered wounds deep and small,

but none worse than the mental wounds inflicted by fear

Don't rock this boat no more

Don't rock this boat no more
Please don't rock this boat again
For we've drifted long in these troubled waters
Now we just can take it no more

The memories we hold are too painful to bear
But we take comfort in this new hope of peace
Though strong winds of anger threaten ugly tides
Land is in sight and we now sail in shallow waters

We've felt this boat rocked from time to time
We've felt the fear, the sorrow and pain
We may not like the ones who steer
But it's a chance we've got and one we're willing to take

So go my friends and tell all Liberians
Tell the angry ones to hold their peace
Tell the weeping ones, we share their pain
Tell the confused ones to watch and wait
Tell them that no one must rock this boat again

Let our sailors join in and help us sail

Let our builders make ready to rebuild our land

Let our teachers get set to teach our children

Let our doctors care for and treat our wounds

But as we steer our boat

Towards land at last

Let no one, I mean no one

Dare rock this boat no more

Full Moon

Tonight must be special
The moon is shining brightly
To waters, she's given new colors
Shining silvery, glistening brightly

Tonight, she's clear and bold
Her body whole, is on display
To people everywhere beneath her light
She's given them reasons more to smile

To evil men who in shadows dwell
Tonight is when they'll moan
For she lightens up their dark shadows
Nowhere to hide, tonight, evil rest

Where now are they?

Where now are they, the voices of resistance?
They, who pressed on with persistence?
Chanting slogans with passion and commitment
Shouting battle cries with relentless vigor?

Where now are they the soldiers of truth?
They, the fighters and champions of the
Down trodden masses?
They who stood fearless and strong
And fought with commitment un-denying?
Where now are they?

They, who struggle, continued in the cause of the people?
They, our revolutionaries
United and consistent in their struggle for change,
Fearless in their quest for peace and justice,
With burning thirst for freedom and liberty
Where now are they?

Thank You Lord

I will praise you Lord
My life, hope, my all
For I'm in a land of strangers
By your Grace, I've known no dangers

In a land so far from home
You've saved my life from doom
I will praise you with all I have
And promise to be well behaved

Out of hunger and war you've brought me
Showing me love and care and what they mean
I ask not why, but I thank You Lord
And I will cling to your Word, my new life's cord.

No more

The day of reckoning is near

When my people, the common people will rise

When against the forces of evil they will rise without fear

At the peril of their own and the lives of those they love

They will shout with the strong voices of unity and of justice

Saying no more Mr. Taylor, No more

No more Mr. Kromah, no more

No more Rosevette Johnson, no more

And you Mr. Boley, we the people say no more

No more will we stand aside and watch our children die

No more will we stand with folded arms and

see our daughters being raped

No more will the people of Liberia stand to see you kill our mothers

and fathers

No more will we stand idly by and watch you abuse and confuse our

children - our precious jewels

No more will we hear your selfish demands

No more will we risk our lives for your selfish aims

This is the day of reckoning, the people will say

The day when we demand the right to our land

The day when we demand justice for the crimes you've committed

We will no longer beg, but demand our freedom, justice and peace

We will no longer feed your ego with our fears

Saah Charles N'Tow

We demand the right to schools for our children

Replacing the barriers of guns with the

powerful but gentle lead of the pencil

No more will we allow your foreign rogues to

steal the wealth of our land

No more will we allow you to plunder our resources,

converting the proceeds to your selfish use

On the day of reckoning, all the people of Liberia will say, no more

Scratching the surface

Most times we stop the fight

But we never stop the war

We change the scene and ease the pain

Mostly wrapping but never healing the wounds

Most times we stop arguments

But we never stop the hatred

We stop insults and ease tensions

Often hiding but never burying the hatchets

Most times we stop the quarrels

But never stop the abuse

We stop the lies and solve one crime

Never really stopping the root of the crime

Saah Charles N'Tow

Blood stained wealth

You smile now because you ride flashy cars
You live in an expensive home
Your family lives abroad
And your children attend foreign schools

But you are no more than a common thief
You are a heartless killer and an ignorant fool
You are a liar, a cheat and a rapist
You killed my people and stole their wealth
My people's blood is the source of your wealth

Thousands are starving while you live in luxury
Yet you will not leave them alone
Thousands are homeless, while you live in a mansion
Yet you will not leave them alone
My people's blood is the source of your wealth

How long will your blood-stained wealth last?
How long can you live with your twisted conscience?
You were once a comrade: trusted and true
Now you have turned a criminal: heartless and cruel
My people's blood is the source of your wealth

You sold our silver and you sold our gold

You sold our diamond and stole our pride

You may laugh now but you won't laugh forever

The people's blood is the source of your wealth

Saah Charles N'Tow

Familiar Strangers

I wish you knew my name
And I wish I knew your name

Strangers together
Victims forever

Shared fate, shared doubts
Little hopes and much pain

Common enemies,
Unspoken trust

We did not plan,
But we worked together

We fought to board the same trucks
Joined lines to beg for food

We shared our hopes and dreams together
We met and cheated death together

We did not know this, but we made our journey together
We met, we struggled and we parted

But I still don't know your name

When it's time

We rode on the strength of the masses
We marched together, boldly

We held our heads up high and proudly
We chanted slogans and battle cries, loudly

It didn't matter, if this march was a crime
We marched together because it was time

When the people march together against injustice
When they finally realize the true extent of their power

When one is all and all is one
They will march together when it is time

We marched together because now was the hour
We the masses realize our true power

We have come to change our fate forever
We march together today because it is time

Saah Charles N'Tow

Sunday will come again

Sunday will come again

These deserted streets will come alive

Laughter of children and parents will fill the air

Fear will fade and joy will gradually return

The church bell will ring again

The pews will be full again

People will serve in joyful obedience

People will dance and sing praises to our God

Sunday will come again

Sunday will come again

When cries of anguish will no longer be heard

And death will find a place elsewhere

Fading light of hope

We who are ambassadors
We who should stand united
In our struggle to seek justice for our people
It is us who now stand divided

Haunted by our indecisions
Plagued by our hatred and selfishness
And limited by our narrow mindedness
We have denied our people

In our division we failed them
Their chances of hope is fading
In us, their light is glowing dimmer
Now in their darkest hour of need
We must rise and truly shine

Deep Water Rising

Deep water rising, river of hate
Deep water rising, changing my fate
Deep water rising, stream of sadness
Deep water rising, I can't swim across

Deep water rising, rising to new levels
Deep water rising, creating new devils
Deep water rising, new depths of fear
Deep water rising, I can't swim across

Deep water rising, destroying my home
Deep water rising, I am among doom
Deep water rising, drowning my children
Deep water rising, I can't swim across

Deep water rising,
Black and white madness
Deep water rising, creating uneasiness
Deep water rising,
Breeding racist nationalists
Deep water rising, I can't swim across

Deep water rising, fading hope

Deep water rising, sliding down life's slope

Deep water rising, everything's floating

Deep water rising, I can't swim across

Deep water rising, but it ain't overflowing

Deep water rising, my courage is growing

Deep water rising, I see new horizons

Deep water rising, I wanna swim across

Deep water rising, storm is subsiding

Deep water rising, water receding

Deep water rising, hopeless but hopeful

Deep water rising, I will swim across

Part IV

Saah Charles N'Tow

Hypocrites in Exile

Open forums, secret meetings
Hidden agenda, evil and cruel
Selfish and greedy power seeking fools
Purchasing positions with my people's blood

So-called patriots in the Diaspora
Blindly searching for some strange miracles
Looking for victories where there are none
In a war without reason that can not be won

So-called leaders living abroad
Inciting violence and fuelling our war
Without remorse you deceive and lie
And misuse our funds to support your ties

Patriots strangely seeking refuge
From a war you started and continue to urge
Heedless to our endless suffering
In our deaths you seek your wealth

I wish you were here

I wish you were here
To feel the heat from the flames
That burnt down the place
I once called my home

I wish you were here
To stand helpless and hopelessly watch
As it disappeared in clouds of smoke
With only remnant of burnt woods and objects to see

I wish you were here
To hear the pleading cries of my family and friends
Begging for mercy: their groans and moans
As they fought to hang on to life
I wish you were here
To hear the mocking laughter of their killers
Mocking and jeering as they watched them die
Sharing tasteless jokes as they committed their heartless crimes

Oh I wish you were here
To see the results of your fundraising campaigns
To see the ruins and relics of your lust for wealth
If for the briefest of moments

Saah Charles N'Tow

God knows that

I wish you were here

The March for change

As if time stood still
And distance did not matter
We rode on the strength of the masses
Fuelled by their anger and want for justice
On this day they were not afraid

They marched together, boldly
They marched together, bravely
They chanted together, loudly
Today was the time
It was time for people's power
It didn't matter, if the things we said rhymed
It didn't matter who among them had charm
Today they marched together

The people of Liberia marched together
Boldly
Bravely
Loudly
Calling on their leaders to step down
Somehow it didn't matter if it was a crime to march the streets

Somehow it didn't matter that the soldiers were well armed

All that mattered was that the people were ready

They had taken to the streets

They marched together boldly

They marched together, bravely

They marched together, courageously

Because today was the people's time

It was time for change

A Stranger's Appeal

Let me not be your fetish sir
For you are my hosts
Your anger I dare not stir
If by chance I dare
My hopes of staying are lost
My sorrow you'll no longer share

Let me not be a burden, sir
Neither must my company, stir up your ire
But tenderly soften your agony
And give rise to peace and harmony

Teach me the laws that govern each dawn
That I may keep them lest you frown
And be then tempted to make a move
That I may certainly not approve

Now Hear This

Children of Africa, rise up
Like the Prophet said, get up and stand up
Use your voices, use your arts, use all you have
Use them to make noises that all can hear

In these lands so far from home
The voices of our brothers and sisters must be heard
Their hurts and suffering must be echoed
Through our writings, through our songs
Through our poems
And through our dances
We must sound our drums and dance our war dances
We must lift our voices and sing our songs
We must rise up against them who kill and abuse
Against them who sell us weapons
Against them whose pleasure it is to watch us die

We must not drift to the dim past of forgotten history
We must not let them thrive on our sufferings
and suppress our progress
We must not let them continue to corrupt our children
and pollute our culture
We must not let them feast on our wealth and our fertile lands

To them we're foreigners unwanted and destructive

Refugees from the war they've created, yet outcasts

Their soldiers discharged, now Worriers in business, Mercenaries!

They won't leave us alone, because it's in our death

that they've found survival

Maybe

If the only images

You see daily are the horrors

Of tragedy and casualties

If the only rest your feet

Can enjoy is the strain

Of endless treks to somewhere safe

If the friends from whom

You are fleeing are the ones

Whose companies you once enjoyed

If the voice of your press

Is silenced by the oppression

Of despotism and tyranny

Who knows?

Maybe you too would be thinking of war

Beyond the playing pitches of South Africa

When all in unity was lost to war?
And the joy of peace faded like a distant dream
When the clouds of terror and grief abound
You stood your ground and fought to bring us pride

In our grief, you made us smile
In our division, you brought us together
Fighters, soldiers, civilians and all
You made us one; you made us proud Liberians again

In your commitment, we found new hope
In your bravery, we found new strength
In your brilliance, we found our pride
In your victories, we found our joy

So, be not dismayed, for you have not lost
You may have lost a trophy, but you've won much more
For beyond the playing pitches of the South African shores
You have a victory compared to none

Saah Charles N'Tow

Back on death row

Temporary relief destroying every belief
That this great country would send my people to roast
Our hopes of living free like the pioneers did
May never come true before Liberians' fate is sealed

Liberians came fleeing a war and its attendant doom
They arrived in America looking for new homes
They found new life, new hope and quests
But it all came crashing down with the loss of TPS

They are seeking refuge, but being refused
They are fleeing death but losing breath
Now it is time to die, the US State Department says
And September 28 is your judgment day

We can help you no more so you must go back home
We know it is not safe, but we've done all we can
We will advise all Americans against traveling to Liberia
Because we know death and suffering await them there

Liberians can return, so they can burn

But Americans must stay cause there's no other way

They say that it's safe for Liberians but not for Americans

So as they wait to know their fate for another year

Liberians are back on death row

Saah Charles N'Tow

I am in your debt

My ever caring and faithful friends
I'm in your debt that knows no end
Suitable superlatives are hard to find
To say how grateful I am to you

I am not surprised my behavior seemed strange
But I can only say, it was out of my range
For I was struggling with stark realities and my pride
Painful and tough, a struggle with too much to hide

Yes, it was much darker than you could see
And I think then, even wider than the sea
But your helping hands and listening ears
Never shied once from my silent pleas

Hence I am in your debt that knows no end
Because, if I have a future I owe it all to you

This poem is dedicated to Anne Metayer and Sabrina Peprino of Paris, France, as well as my friend and brother Alberto Lo Gioco of Udine, Italy. During the early years of my troubles, they stood by, supported and tried their best to comfort me. Years have gone now and they may have deposited me in the fading past of their memories, but if I have a future now, they all had a part to play in it. They believed in me. With this poem, I wish to thank them, and through them their families, AIESEC EDHEC of LILLE, AIESEC Zagreb, AIESEC Sierra Leone, AIESEC Italy, etc..

A Book of your mind

If your mind was a book I could read
With a cover and pages that I could turn
If its chapters unveil thoughts and feelings untold
What chills or thrills, will its plots unfold?

If it tells the story of your here and now
Of the how and why, the when and where
If its title says it all in just one word
How revealing or suggestive will it be?

If it tells of your past, deep secrets unknown
Of fear and pain or sadness and joy unrefined
If it reveals those plots and plans, hidden deep
Will the shock be pleasant or terribly sad?

If it tells of the love and hate in your life
Of your friends and foes, both far and near
If it tells of those moments, both happy and sad
Will the reflections unlock joy or painful tears?

My Beleaguered People

They have been down so long

They are conditioned to accept all wrongs

They accept that corruption cannot change

Because change is never within their range

They are strong but feel helpless

They are divided, but remain clueless

They are conditioned to live in division

While resisting unity: their ultimate protection

They are many, but remain afraid

They are controlled by alerts and constant code red

They fear the weapon of their suppressors

Blindly trusting, they aid his conniving wicked successors

Through those long years

Flipping through the pages of my past
I cannot help but wonder
About the places,
The people, and all the things I passed

I wonder about my journey, my escape to safety at last
I wonder about the times of pain and the times of shame
Though I know that no magic of time or memories
Can bring back my joy or fears
I cannot help, but wonder still, if really I did make it
through those long years

Face to face with death one too many times
I've been a victim of hostilities and one too many crimes
Creeping and crawling through bushes and alleys
I was unable to shout or scream or even struggle in terror's valley

And when I saw the best amongst us reduced to dust
I felt then, that dying for me was most certainly a matter of must
Now, for all the good and bad memories
That remain so vivid and clear
I cannot help, but wonder still, if really I did make it
through those long years

What's left of you in these violent times?

Land of liberty of yester years:
Liberia, land of pasture green, the grain coast of Africa
Richness in abundance with the gifts of the Earth
Iron ore, gold, diamond and beautiful green forest
O land of my birth, for which I eagerly crave
What's left of you in these violent times?

Fresh ocean winds cooling your nights
Bright shining sun, warming your busy breezy days
Heavenly showers watering your grain and fertile soil
Your rivers full of riches: natural and abundant
O my beloved country of which I constantly dream
What's left of you in these violent times?

Gazing cattle, wildlife and games
Wonderful tones from the beautiful birds of your skies
You are naturally blessed with the gifts of the gods
The gift of two seasons: raining and dry
O my motherland: my very own land, my pride
What's left of you in these violent times?

Before the buildings fell

Before the building fell, we were gaining ground
We struggled hard, but we were winning crowns

Before the buildings fell we had lots of friends
Our cultures and costumes simply did not offend

Before the buildings fell, we were people many respected
Our religion, origin, class or creed were never ever inspected

Before the buildings fell, our clothes or language made no difference
In school, our children's clothes or accent was never cause for
severance

But when the buildings fell, our hopes came tumbling down
In our fight we started loosing ground

After the buildings fell, our friends became our foes
Suddenly, we were different from head to toe

Saah Charles N'Tow

After the buildings fell, they no longer came to but, ran from us

Where even little love once lived

there was nothing but lack of trust

After the buildings fell, champions of hate rule the land

It is finally working: their conniving and evil plan

Towards Reconciliation

How can we forgive?

Such intentional crimes against our people?

How can we forget?

The scars and wounds that stare at us everyday?

How can we turn the other cheek?

When there is simply none to turn?

How can we extend a hand of peace

When there is no hand left to extend?

Who will erase the memories of our pain and suffering?

Who will heal the wounds of the pain we bore?

Who will bring back the laughter we once knew?

Who will bring back our families and rebuild our homes?

Are these not the same ones, who brought us death and destruction?

Are they not the same ones who smiled

as they rapped and killed our children?

Are they not the same ones who forced us to smile

as they tore off our body parts?

Are they not the same ones who knew not the meaning of mercy?

Saah Charles N'Tow

How can you ask me to trust you?

You who left me for dead?

How can you ask me to trust you?

You who tore my family apart?

How can you ask me to trust you?

You who once thirsted after my blood?

Message to my family

If you see my family,

Please greet them for me

Tell the ones you see that I miss them so

Remember the faces you see

And tell me how they are

But ask nothing about the

Ones you do not see

If you meet my mother,

Please tell her I am still alive

Tell her kindly to wait for me

Remember to tell her I love her so

But ask her nothing

About how she survived

Choice?

No one leaves was the order

He or she who tries to leave is the enemy

The enemy must die

Enemies of the state must be killed

Stay and be ruled by the hands of terror

Stay and flirt with danger and death

Stay and wait for the next order

Stay and face uncertainty and fear

Or meet your fate in flight

We are one

From countries and cultures far across the sea
We have to come make our homes here
Different languages, cultures and tribes
We are stronger together
Because we are one!

We bring the wealth of culture and the gifts of friendship
We come willing to learn, as we have come to share
Our sons and daughters, our neighbors and friends
We can live better together
When we are one!

Stressing our differences is not our preference
We come to build strong bridges to bring us closer
Though the gaps of prejudices and hatred widen each day
We can build bridges and cross them together
If we work as one!

Liberians for Peace and Reconstruction make you this pledge
That from the highest hills of our differences
To the selective hurdles of our respective preferences
We will search for the strings that tied us together
As we work together to make us all one!

Mr. Minister in waiting

Mr. Minister in waiting
Making sure your men are fighting
Watching and waiting for your calling
Even at the cost of your people dying

Mr. Minister in waiting
Bankrolling the cause of our destroyers
Pretending you are the sympathizers
The peace-loving wolf in sheep's clothing

Mr. Minister in waiting
The mastermind: the real killer
Selling our country to gain your wealth
Your life, your wealth, your people's deaths

Mr. Minister in waiting
So-called patriot in hiding
Spilling the blood of the innocents
In exchange for your useless dollars and cents

Choose Peace

No one wins a war
No one survives its impact
Illusions of victories may feed our ego
But the realities of our action will hunt us forever

Everyone is a victim of blasting bombs and smoking guns
Cause they destroy our flesh, our minds and homes
Even the ones who drop bombs and shoot guns
Suffer wounds that scar their lives forever

War is often fought between two strangers
But all feel the impact of war
The young, the old, the weak and strong
Even the victors lose their pound of flesh in war

Dead bodies, broken hearts and homes
And strangers turned enemies fuelled by perennial hatred
Leave horrible monuments of war in their path
Because war hurts and helps neither victor or victims

Saah Charles N'Tow

War is never necessary

No war is ever justified

For the many lives and homes we stand to lose

I hope our leaders will always

Choose peace

A Resettled Child's Song

Thanks a million for getting me out
Out of a world of terror and war
I am grateful
I really am, but
There is a lot about me you do not know

I am not the same little kid you left behind
The one who got lost and was hard to find
It's been a little while since you last saw me
I may look the same, but
There is a lot about me you do not know

In those missing years, I had to endure
The pain of separation and growing up alone
You were not there to help me grow
I love you, I really do, but
There is a lot about you do not know

You drop me off at school and drive away
Not a thought on how my troubled days are spent
I know you care, I know you really do
Come on let's be real
There is a lot about me you do not know

119

Saah Charles N'Tow

You pay the rent and buy the food

You even buy clothes and leave me some change

I see the change, the clothes and food

I understand you work but I still need you, because

There is a lot about me you do not know

I know you expect me to do my best

Work hard in school and ace my tests

It has been a long time since I was last in school

In class I look different, sound different and feel like a fool

Daddy before it gets too late, we need to talk, because

There is a lot about me you do not know

Future Challenge: The WAR CHILD

How do you explain peace to a child born in war?
How do you talk about trust when hatred is all she knows?
How do you talk about RIGHTS when WRONGS abound?
How do you describe tomorrow, when today is such a mess?

How do you describe joy to an embittered child?
A child accustomed to unrivaled horror and hatred?
How do you describe a home to a child living in war?
When life in temporary camps is so routine and real

What do you say about having a family in the midst of chaos?
When the family he knows is his user and abuser?
When do you tell her about respect and love?
When slavery and sex are the reasons she is kept alive?

What do you say about life and its attendant joy?
When body counts are the only joys he is taught to share?
What do you tell him about school, play and work?
Amidst the heartless carnage and devastation around

How can you describe trust?

When trusting no one is a matter of must?

What you do say about friendship?

When the best friend he has is the weapon he carries?

What do you tell her about hope?

When all her life feels like sliding down a slope?

How do you tell her she is a child: a beautiful child?

When her beauty and age have brought her so much pain?

How do you talk about peace, joy, hope or love?

What do you say about RIGHTS, friendship or family?

How do you talk about life, school, play or work?

How do you talk about peace?

To a child born in war?

Part V

Saah Charles N'Tow

I want to vote too

I am a citizen
I am from Lofa
My county is bleeding
My children are dying
My family is being terrorized
As you talk about elections

I know you have set the date, the time and place
I know we are in a hurry to change the status quo
Like the one before, impatience now rules the day
I know we are ready to settle for anything

But before you get too excited
Please know this
I want to vote too

What about me?

Could you spare a minute for me?
I won't keep you long: I have to run anyway
The soldiers will soon be back to hunt me
So forgive my insistence but I must speak now
Since I am not sure if I will be alive after today

By way of introduction, my name is Lofa County
I am a part of a family called Liberia
Which ironically means "liberty"
Right now I feel anything but liberated

In my little makeshift hideout not far from home
A weary traveler spoke about elections
Amidst the flying bullets and broken homes
We sat around to listen to his every word

He spoke about a new buzz in Monrovia about elections
Liberians are excited, he said about new possibilities
Liberians are excited about old politicians with new plans
Liberians are excited about an election for new leaders

We had many questions he couldn't answer
We had many suggestions he wouldn't take

125

We wanted participation he couldn't guarantee

We wanted assurances he couldn't give

Because he, like all of us, was on the run from death

Maybe I missed this on the news

Or maybe I missed this in the paper

You see I'm in hiding and can't play my radio

And the papers: they don't come out anymore

Since the publishers are dead or on the run

All this talk about elections, is someone thinking about me?

I may not live till tomorrow, but will my family be allowed to vote?

Will my scattered children and terrified family ever feel safe to vote?

Oh candidates for our highest office

If this is an election for our leaders, please tell me

What about me?

A dying citizen's wish

If you are reading this then my death is not in vain
Because this is the last thing I have the chance to do before I die
Soldiers are waiting outside for the final orders to kill me
I have exhausted the one and final appeal I had
Death is certain and it is no longer a choice

But before I am undressed, spat at and humiliated
Before I am marched to the spot of my execution
Before I'm shot, cut up or buried alive
I have decided to write and ask you this

Will my family feel safe to vote?
With flying bullets and hungry killers
Looting fighters, raping and destroying my home
Where will you put my voting booths?

Since the invasion and the destruction of my home
Since I lost my family and got on the run
Since greedy fighters came looting and killing
Hope of peace is the last thing on my mind

Saah Charles N'Tow

But even in death as I listen to my killers talk
My fear of death is fading fast
For I have overheard one of my killers say
There is rumor in the air about an election soon

What you are now reading is my dying wish
Do not forbid my family because of this war
If the leaders you elect are to lead them too
Then I wish today as I wait to die
That my family in Lofa be allowed to vote!

Not this time!

Violence for power
Not this time

Destroying our country
Not this time

Another year with Taylor
Not this time

Human rights abuses
Not this time

Greed-driven insurgence
Not this time

Blind rage, more revenge
Not this time

More depots in power
Not this time

Terrorizing our people
Not this time

Runaway ministers returning with new armies
Not this time

Old politicians with new tricks
Not this time

"You kill my ma, you kill my pa, I will vote for you?"
Not this time

Together, the people of Liberia are saying
NOT THIS TIME

Not This Time (II)

No more rewards for violence
No more greed-driven insurgence
This Liberia is our very own country
We will not loose it to endless banditry
Not this time

Warlords have killed us and destroyed our lands
As part of their scheming and conniving plans
So for us who have lived to see this day,
We must not allow them to have their way
Not this time

We must demand our place at the peace table
And add our voices to help make our country stable
No more fragile agreements to please our tormentors
For we must not pretend that they are not murderers
Not this time

LURD, MODEL, Taylor or whatever your affiliations
We demand immediate cessation of any further destruction
Trickery, banditry and greed will not conquer
The hope of peace and stability offered by this new accord
Not this time

Saah Charles N'Tow

Thinking about You

The night was long and I couldn't sleep
I couldn't sleep cause I was thinking deep
I was thinking deep, but only about you
I was thinking about you, you and only you

I was thinking about the moments we shared together
Our hopes and dreams in a timeless heaven
You weren't here: I wasn't there, but I felt good
Cause I was thinking about you, you and only you

I was thinking about the moment: that brief moment
When our hearts and minds were locked in silent torment
It was a kiss in fear: it was short, sweet and good
Because it came from you, you and only you

Awake

The tears I feel now fill my eyes
Another pain, another loss, another broken heart
For I wake this day from a sweet, sweet dream
A dream so sweet, I want to dream again

It was lovely dream, I found love again
Having suffered long: the pain of a broken heart
I saw a beauty that consumed my thoughts
A beauty so rare, my heart I lost

In that dream I saw no walls
No distance or color nor culture to stall
I felt one thing: it was natural love
Endless and true: too real to prove

Now it is gone and it is suddenly clear
Distance and culture and all I feared
A rather quick dream, but one very dear
If I could have my way,
I would wish it were real

My Preference

Distance, culture, people and work
Tend to draw us both far apart
But the more I give this a serious thought
The closer you get to my heart

You are closer to me than you will ever know
And I hope for the chance one day to show
That distance and culture do make some difference
But for me you will always be my preference

It has been a long time now since I felt this way
A feeling of passion, comfort and peace
Call it friendship or whatever you may
But for me you will always be my missing piece

Silent Admirer

I stood spellbound as I watched you dance
Enjoying the grace and elegance with which you moved
I quietly hoped to steal your glance
But I lost you to the rhythm of the grove

As your dazzling beauty made many heads turn
The stirs you caused: words cannot explain
Your charming smiles made many hearts yearn
Each silently wishing you would be his queen

Saah Charles N'Tow

It all happened to me

Roving about the streets each day
And always looking for trouble
I never thought that I would one day
Sit and say, it all happened to me

From the needle to the bottle
Getting too high and getting too drunk
I never thought I would one day manage
To say, it all happened to me

From jail cell to jail cell, lashes upon lashes
There was no hope of relief for me
I never dreamt of one day being able
To say, it all happened to me

While people entered through doors but I entered through windows,
looking for what I called a living
Years have passed and so have my fears
For the winds of change have dried my tears
I am glad and blessed today
To say, it all happened to me

The Paradox of Intimacy

I think that

It matters not for how long we met

Nor the place, the time or things we shared

What matters most is that we met

We met, we shared and we are glad we did

Now

Your silence speaks volumes to me

Your absence is a presence so strong

In the distance, I feel you close

In the darkness of your absence, I still see your face

Because

I hear you, when you don't talk

I talk to you, though you are not listening

I feel you, though you are not here

I touch you, when I don't

I miss you!

Searching For Real Leaders

Who will be our leaders in these troubled times?

And resist the temptation to commit further crimes

Who will rise above self-interest, ego and personal aggrandizement?

To represent the cause of our people and restore their contentment

Who will be the peacemakers in these opportune times?

When the whole world is watching and waiting for changing signs

Who will be the negotiators at a time when we need them most?

And not be that delegate who is seeking some new government post

Who will speak with the fairness that leaves no party behind?

Respects and is respected by all:

One who is committed, truthful and kind?

Who will see our country through the eyes of the dove of peace?

Seeing one Liberia, one people and the need for violence to cease

Who will help us control our rage in such angry times?

And not use our blind rage as an excuse to launch another attack

Who will fly to the peace table in Ghana to help solve our problems?

And not look for new opportunities to destroy and kill our people

Who really cares about Liberia, enough to forego revenge?

Who is willing to do anything to bring this foolishness to an end?

Who will suppress his own to seek the interest of all Liberians?

Who will give up the guns for the ballots of true democracy?

Who will be our leaders in these troubled times?

Saah Charles N'Tow

Beleaguered People

We have been down so long
We are conditioned to accept all wrongs
We accept that corruption cannot change
Because change is never within our range

We are strong but feel helpless
We are divided, but remain clueless
We are conditioned to live in division
While resisting unity: our ultimate protection

We are many, but remain afraid
We are controlled by code reds and constant alerts
We fear the weapon of our suppressors
Blindly trusting, we aid his conniving wicked successors

About the Author

Saah C. N'Tow is one of Africa's brilliant upcoming young poets. He is a community organizer, a peace activist and a founding member and a former leader of the Liberian Community Organization (LICO). He worked with the Liberian Community Association of Rhode Island (LCARI) as its Development and Immigration Committees chair (1998–2003). In 2001, he was awarded a Rhode Island Foundation Fellowship to promote poetry as therapy in post war societies.

He holds a Bachelor of Science in Mathematics (University of Liberia); a Masters of Science in Human Services Administration from (Springfield College, MA); and a Postgraduate Certificate in Youth and Community Services from Brunel University (Middlesex, England).

Saah has shared his powerfully moving poems with large and small audiences in the UK, Holland, Africa and the USA. He was a guest on the BBC (once on Network Africa and twice on the Art House program, in 1997) broadcasting to millions of listeners all around Africa and the rest of the world. The author lives with his wife, Symbu and three children in Providence, Rhode Island.